SYLVANUS THAYER 1808 • JEFFERSON DAVIS 1828 • ROBERT EDWARD LEE 1829 • WILLIAM TECUMSEH SHERMAN 1840 • ABNER DOUBLEDAY 1842 • ULYSSES SIMPSON GRANT 1843 • GEORGE BRINTON MC CLELLAN 1846 • GEORGE EDWARD PICKETT 1846 • THOMAS JONATHAN JACKSON 1846 • GEORGE CROOK 1852 • PHILLIP HENRY SHERIDAN 1853 • JAMES EWELL BROWN STUART 1854 • GEORGE ARMSTRONG CUSTER 1861 • RANALD SLIDELL MACKENZIE 1862 • GEORGE WASHINGTON GOETHALS 1880 • JOHN JOSEPH PERSHING 1886 •

THE TRADITION

PEYTON CONWAY MARCH 1888 • CHARLES P. SUMMERALL 1892 • ROBERT E. WOOD 1900 • DOUGLAS MACARTHUR 1903 • JOSEPH WARREN STILWELL 1904 • JONATHAN MAYHEW WAINWRIGHT 1906 • HENRY HARLEY ARNOLD 1907 • GEORGE SMITH PATTON, JR. 1909 • CARL SPAATZ 1914 • DWIGHT DAVID EISENHOWER 1915 • JAMES ALWARD VAN FLEET 1915 • OMAR NELSON BRADLEY 1915 • ROBERT REESE NEYLAND, JR. 1916 • MARK WAYNE CLARK 1917 • MATTHEW BUNKER RIDGWAY 1917 • LESLIE RICHARD GROVES 1918 • LUCIUS DU BIGNON CLAY 1918 • ALBERT COADY WEDEMEYER 1919 • ALFRED MAXIMILLIAN GRUENTHER 1919 • NATHAN FARRAGUT TWINING 1919 • LYMAN LOUIS LEMNITZER 1920 • MAXWELL DAVENPORT TAYLOR 1922 • FRANK DOW MERRILL 1929 • EARLE GILMORE WHEELER 1932 • WILLIAM ORLANDO DARBY 1933 • CREIGHTON W. ABRAMS, JR. 1936 • COLIN P. KELLY, JR. 1937 • GEORGE BROWN 1941

DUTY

HONOR

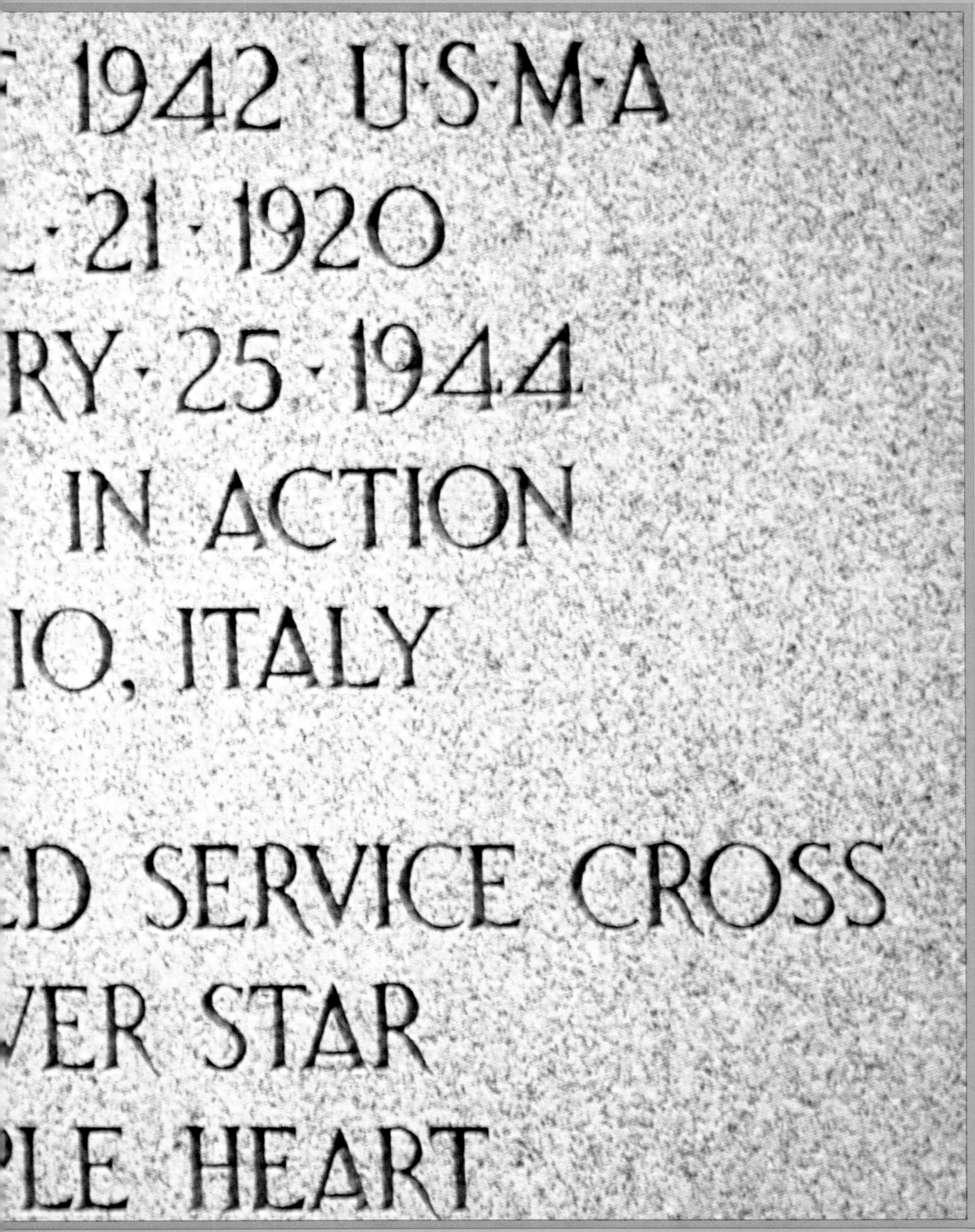

1942 U·S·M·A

21·1920

25·1944

IN ACTION

IO, ITALY

ED SERVICE CROSS

ER STAR

LE HEART

COUNTRY

WEST POINT

UNITED STATES MILITARY ACADEMY

1802

PHOTOGRAPHED BY BOB KRIST

HARMONY HOUSE
PUBLISHERS LOUISVILLE

...along a glittering path of sunlit water with here and there a skiff, whose white sail often bends on some new track as sudden flows of wind come down upon her from the gullies in the hills; hemmed in, besides, all 'round with memories of Washington, and events of the Revolutionary War: is the Military School of America. It could not stand on more appropriate ground, and any ground more beautiful can hardly be. The course of education is severe, but well-devised and manly.

Charles Dickens, *American Notes*, 1841

Cullum Hall

First Printing Fall 1987 by Harmony House Publishers
P.O. Box 90, Prospect, Kentucky 40059 (502) 228-2010/ 228-4446
Executive Editors: William Butler and William Strode
Director of Photography: William Strode
Hardcover International Standard Book Number 0-916509-16-8
Library of Congress Catalog Number 86-082738
Copyright © 1987 by Harmony House Publishers
Photographs © 1987 by Robert Krist

Harmony House extends thanks and sincere appreciation
to the Association of Graduates, United States Military
Academy, for its efforts in making this publication possible.

Headquarters, United States Military Academy

And be it enacted that the said corps, when so organized shall be stationed at West Point in the state of New York, and shall constitute a military academy.

An Act of the 7th Congress of the United States, directed by Thomas Jefferson, 1802

FOREWORD

The story of West Point parallels that of America. Beginning as a craggy fortress built where granite-edged mountains squeeze the broad Hudson River into a narrow, tortuous gorge, it was the strategic center of the War of Independence. George Washington camped the Continental Army either right here or nearby, rarely marching far away and always returning as soon as he could. Today, links to our Revolutionary War heritage stand in honored presence all about the grounds – a treasure store marking our Nation's birth.

Our newly independent country retained its Army "to provide for the common defense." The nature of the young American republic demanded officers with democratic values and unquestioned character. To meet this need, Thomas Jefferson founded the Military Academy in 1802. As the Nation has matured, this need has endured. More than ever, our military leaders must be exemplars of the values that frame the Nation; West Point is the wellspring of these values.

A special trust sets the Military Academy apart from all other educational institutions in this land: its mission is to educate and train the Corps of Cadets so that each graduate shall have the attributes essential to professional growth in the Regular Army, and to inspire each to a lifetime of service to the Nation.

The world renowned West Point experience is the essence of the Academy's uniqueness. It begins at the very moment of arrival for each new cadet, including, on that first day, a solemn oath to support the Constitution. Four years later, as the graduate prepares to don Army Green, an oath is again taken — this time to support *and defend* the Constitution.

Transformation from eager new cadet to inspired new leader is a complex passage. The compass for this arduous journey is the simple but great moral code – Duty, Honor, Country. This powerful expression of the ethos of the American soldier shapes from the outset the very fiber of those who undergo the West Point experience. The passage is marked and measured along three distinct but intertwined roads: intellectual, physical, and military development. These roads are required travel for each cadet. Along the way, in an all-encompassing and absorbing process, the Academy's spartan lifestyle and sustaining environment carefully nurture the development of character. Omnipresent in that environment are an abiding emphasis on a moral-ethical code, demanding discipline, a proud linkage to tradition, and a climate promoting social growth.

Ultimately this experience, this process of forging and growth, occurring within this matchless environment, produces leaders of character and forms their enduring foundation of dedicated service to country. It has been so for nearly two centuries now.

Ghosts walk the Plain at West Point. Hallowed spirits of men who mapped and made America, who fought our country's battles, who led the way at every juncture, to include the leap into space. Grant and Lee, Pershing and Patton, Eisenhower and MacArthur – warrior names. Frank Borman, Edward White, Edwin Aldrin – astronaut names. At West Point, you see, much of the history we teach was made by those we taught. They are the Long Gray Line.

Read through the pages of this book. Then come walk these storied acres. Your heart will beat stronger, your step will gain extra spring, your head will tilt higher – for you will have savored a return to the very source of the values on which our Nation was built.

Dave R. Palmer
Lieutenant General, U.S. Army
Superintendent
United States Military Academy

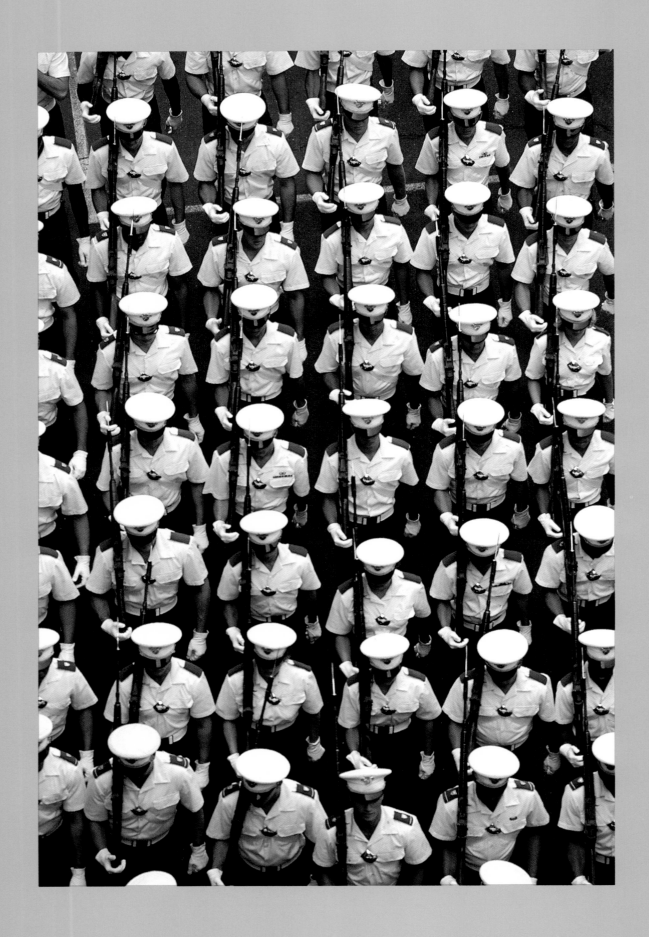

INTRODUCTION

General William T. Sherman
Commencement Address, 1869

My Young Friends:

I am here this day at the invitation of your superintendent, and in pursuance of an honored custom, to add by my official presence to the interest of an occasion that has brought together so many of your friends. Your academic term of life is now over; the day for which you have waited so long has come at last, and you are about to sally forth into the wide, wide world, to a large extent masters of your own actions, to bear its burdens and to enjoy its fruits. The diplomas this day conferred on you, and which you have fairly earned, are the official testimony prescribed by law, recorded on parchment, and verified by the signatures of your professors, certifying that you are qualified to be commissioned as officers in the Army of the United States.

Twenty-nine long years have passed since I stood where you do now, yet the feelings and emotions of that epoch of life come back with these familiar scenes so clear and distinct, that I feel strongly inclined to cut short the few words I had prepared for the occasion, and to bid you fly to the loved ones at home that await your coming. Even now, I shall not delay you long, nor say one word calculated to moderate the natural feelings of relief that the restraints hitherto imposed are relaxed, that your books are cast aside for a time, and that you are substantially free. I hope that each and every one of you will enjoy to its fullest extent the furlough of three months that awaits you; and as it draws to a conclusion, I only beg you to pause a moment and consider the kindly offerings of those who have already trodden the same path on which you are so impatient to enter, so that when you reach the first posts of duty, you may be prepared to lay a sure foundation for a life of usefulness and honor for yourselves, and to pay back to your Government in services for the great advantages you have received here.

Your professors now certify that you are proficient in all the studies deemed necessary to a military education, and your superintendent will tell me your general standing which determines your first rank in the army. I have not the least doubt that each and every one of you can solve all the problems of the triangle, that you can measure the solid contents of cubes and spheres, and some of you may even calculate all the phases of the eclipse of the sun expected next August; but there is a great problem in which you and I, and all the world, have a deep interest, and which neither superintendent nor professor will attempt to unfold. I mean the great problem of life, when no kind teacher will be at your elbow to prompt and interpret for you, and wherein the variable and unknown quantities exceed in number the letters of the Greek alphabet. What is to be your fate in the unknown future? What sort of officers will you make?

Fortunately or unfortunately, as the case may be,

General Dwight D. Eisenhower

you are not compelled, like many a poor fellow, to grope in the dark for a new profession or the means of livelihood. Your Government has already provided for you in advance an honorable station, with a code of laws and regulations so plain and easy that all may understand. It has taken you in youth, with the full consent of your parents, and has given you an education and training at public cost, that you may serve it and dedicate your life and best labours in manhood to it, with the promise of an honorable maintenance in sickness and old age. You will now be called on to confirm and ratify the act of your parents, to dedicate yourselves anew to the service of your country, and, to certain extent, to surrender a large proportion of that natural liberty of action which all Americans prize so highly. Still you are untrammeled, each for himself to choose your own course of action, and to shape your

own destiny. The limits within which you are free to act may seem narrow to an ambitious youth; yet as you advance you will find room and verge enough for the display of a reasonable amount of energy and talents. Should any of you, however, think differently, now is the time to choose from among the various callings open to all in this favored land of ours, a profession suited to your own taste and inclinations, and I feel certain your countrymen will not begrudge you the boon of a public education, provided only you carry into civil life that sense of honor and integrity which we claim to be characteristic of the military profession.

I take it for granted the great mass of the class now before me will, like their predecessors, pass into the regular army, full of hope and ambition, determined to seek the bubble Fame at the cannon's mouth, and resolved to reach the topmost round of its ladder. To these I shall be most happy in after-life to extend a helping hand, if you need it, but at this moment I need only offer you that cheapest gift of man, Advice.

To be good officers you must be good men, true, faithful, honest, honorable, sober, industrious, and above all you must love your country, and your profession, with an ardor in comparison with which every other feeling will pale as the rush-light in the sun. The knight of old was said to be wedded to his sword; this should be emblematic of the modern soldier, who should love his corps, his regiment, and his company, so that separation would be as banishment. For many years you must be content with subordinate positions, but even then you will have an admirable opportunity to study, not only from books, but from the acts and examples of your seniors, and you may even profit by their mistakes. Step by step, you must rise as older men pass away, and you should be well prepared for each change when it comes. Many and many a time will you realize that you have to sacrifice your best feelings, your strongest convictions, your comfort, your safety, even life itself, for your country or in the interests of others, and you may have to bear in silence the flings and taunts of personal enemies, the coldness and aversion of supposed friends, and the malediction of men whose interests you are compelled to cross; but you must go on, surmounting with a steady hand the dangers and difficulties as they arise, watch well the currents which mark the world's progress, keep as far as you can in the main channel of events; and be very careful lest, in search of present ease and immediate advantage, you may drift into some side eddy, there to whirl about like a useless piece of drift-wood. Let your thoughts and aim always keep in view some practical, useful end. I know that there exist many good men who honestly believe that one may, by the aid of modern science, sit in comfort and ease in his office chair, and with little blocks of wood to represent men, or even

with figures and algebraic symbols, master the great game of war. I think this an insidious and most dangerous mistake.

Science may test to a pound the strain on every chord, and brace, and rod of the most complicated structure, or it may separate the component parts of every mineral; but it cannot penetrate the hearts of men. The soldier in the ranks is not a block of wood or a nerve unit; he is a man like yourselves, full of feeling and passion, varying in size, and strength, and all the attributes of manhood. As one man varies from another, so bodies of men vary still more, whilst certain characteristics pervade them all.

The only schools where war and its kindred sciences can be popularly learned are in the camp, in the field, on the plains, in the mountains, or at the regular forts where the army is. You must understand men, without which your past knowledge were vain. You must come into absolute contact with soldiers, partake of their food and labors, share their vicissitudes, study their habits, impress yourself on them and be impressed by them, until they realize that you not only possess more book knowledge than they, but that you equal, if not surpass them, in all the qualities of manhood — in riding, in swimming, in enduring the march and bivouac, in the sagacity of the woodman and hunter; and, what is most important of all, you must acquire that great secret of human control by which masses of men are led to deeds of infinite courage and heroism.

Rome was great and glorious when her legions could march their ten leagues a day, and carry their fifty pounds of baggage per man; when her proudest consuls sought honor at the head of those legions in the forests of Transalpine Gaul and Germany. But she declined when those same consuls sought ease and luxury in her marble palaces, or in those exquisite villas which her poets and philosophers made immortal.

India and the colonies have been to England a rare

school for Generals; and the national sports of riding, and hunting, and yachting, have preserved the physical superiority of her youth in spite of the home comforts and luxuries of the great mass of her people.

No modern nation possesses better military academies than France; yet the barren wastes and steppes of Algeria have trained some of her best modern Generals.

In our favored country you have every stimulus possible to develop the manly strength and courage so essential to success in our chosen profession of arms. The whole sea-coast and Northern lakes invite you to out-door exercise in boating and fishing. The waters of Florida and Texas swarm with fish, and their woods and fields abound in deer and wild game. The great plains are lively with the Sioux, the Cheyennes, and Arapahoes, and the vast herds of buffalo, of which you have heard so much. The Rocky Mountains still afford an endless range to the mountain sheep, the blacktail deer, the elk and antelope; and the far-off mountains of California, Oregon and Idaho, will nurture for many a year to come, enough grizzly and cinnamon bears to dare to the encounter the boldest rider and hunter.

These are the schools in which you are destined to learn many a hard lesson of patience and endurance, and it is from these schools that I look for the men who are to lead our future armies. I have oftentimes been asked by friends, familiar with Xenophon, Hume, and Jomini, in which of these books I had learned the secret of leading armies on long and difficult marches, and they seemed surprised when I answered that I was not aware that I had been influenced by any of them. I told them what I now tell you in all simplicity and truth, that when I was a young lieutenant of artillery, I had often hunted deer in the swamps of the Edisto, the Cooper, and the Santee, and had seen with my own eyes that they could be passed with wagons; that in the spring of 1844, I had ridden on horseback from Marietta, Georgia, to the Valley of the Tennessee and back

to Augusta, passing in my course over the very fields of Altoona, of Kenesaw, and Atlanta, when afterwards it fell to my share to command armies, and to utilize the knowledge thus casually gained: again, in 1849 and 1850, I was in California, and saw arrive the caravans of emigrants, composed of men, women, and children, who reached their destination in health and strength, having crossed that wide belt of two thousand miles of uninhabited country; and we would start on a journey of a thousand miles with a single blanket as covering, and a coil of dried meat and a sack of parched corn-meal as food. With this knowledge fairly acquired in actual experience, was there any need for me to look back to Alexander the Great, to Marlborough, or Napoleon, as examples? Would I not rather have been worthy of censure had I hesitated when duty called, to conduct a well-organized army, thoroughly equipped and abundantly supplied, across the few hundred miles of inhabited country that lay between me and the enemies of our Government?

There was an old army rule, that every officer should serve with his company for at least three years before ever asking for a leave of absence or for a staff detail. This rule was founded in experience dating far back in the history of our ancestors, and for this rule I entertain a profound respect that some of you may have occasion to complain of hereafter; but I honestly believe that, great and important as have been the lessons you have learned at West Point, those you must acquire in the first four years of actual service in the army will be equally important, and will have a more direct influence on your individual fame and fortunes. Do not understand me as undervaluing education in any form, especially in the manner pursued here, or that which results from a careful study of history and precedents; but that I attach equal importance to that practical knowledge that can only be acquired by actual contact with men in camp, on the picket line, and on the march, as also in the administra-

Battle Monument

tion of affairs by which an army is enlisted, organized, clothed, equipped, fed, paid and handled in battle.

If any one of you were suddenly called on to manage a steam-engine, in perfect order, I doubt if you would like to undertake it, though you profess to understand the function of all its parts and the principles of science by which they are governed.

An army is a much more complicated machine than a steam engine. It is composed of an infinite variety of parts, each unit being of flesh and blood, requiring food and clothing, arms, ammunition, wagons, tents, and almost everything natural and manufactured. It is held together by an organization and discipline demanding great knowledge and labor, moved into action by causes more powerful than steam, and so intimately connected with the whole fabric of government, that ignorance and mismanagement would result in a catastrophe more fatal than could result from the explosion of any steam engine. Even in a time of peace and equilibrium, an army demands the watchful care of trained and skillful officers; and when aroused to action, it calls for the exercise of the highest qualities of human nature, enlightened by study and fortified by the experience of a lifetime. You may hear of men born as generals, but I have yet to see the first one who has not been compelled to earn his fame by hard study, toil and exposure, and I should as soon look for an experienced surgeon among students, or a lawyer fit to manage a case in the Supreme Court of the United States who had not passed through a long training in the inferior Courts, as to find an officer fit to command an army in the field, who had not passed the ordeal in the minor grades of our profession.

Of course an army may be used, and is constantly used, in connection with the civil administration of government; yet war is its true element, and battle its ultimate use. The habits of its component parts should be shaped to that end, more especially in time of peace, when there are so many disturbing causes at work, and when the pretensions and boasts of men cannot be subjected to that stern test which so promptly proves the true from the false.

Many of you may lead a long and active life without witnessing a great battle, or even engaging in mortal strife; yet if it come upon you and find you unprepared, you will surely be adjudged derelict and condemned accordingly. I hope, therefore, that you realize that you have only begun the study and labor of your profession; that you have only acquired by four years of hard study at West Point, a partial use of its rudiments. Yet these rudiments are deemed by all men, civilians as well as soldiers, so important, that the Government of the United States has founded this National Academy at great cost, and has maintained it for more than fifty years, through good report and through evil report; and I believe it will continue to foster and support it, if the graduates will, as heretofore, display in their lives the virtues common to all professions, and especially that ardent, deep devotion to our National Flag which has made it a proud emblem over the whole surface of this globe.

And now, my young friends, I will conclude by repeating that your run in the great contest of life has only begun; that your country now offers you an honorable career, with the highest honors to him who will labor hard to deserve them. No matter what your standing may be in your class, you start again fair and square in a race where perseverance in the right will surely win, and you may rest assured that your ultimate fate and fame will result from the laws of God — designed for living men as wise and beneficent, and far more intricate than those which guide the dead planets in their spheres.

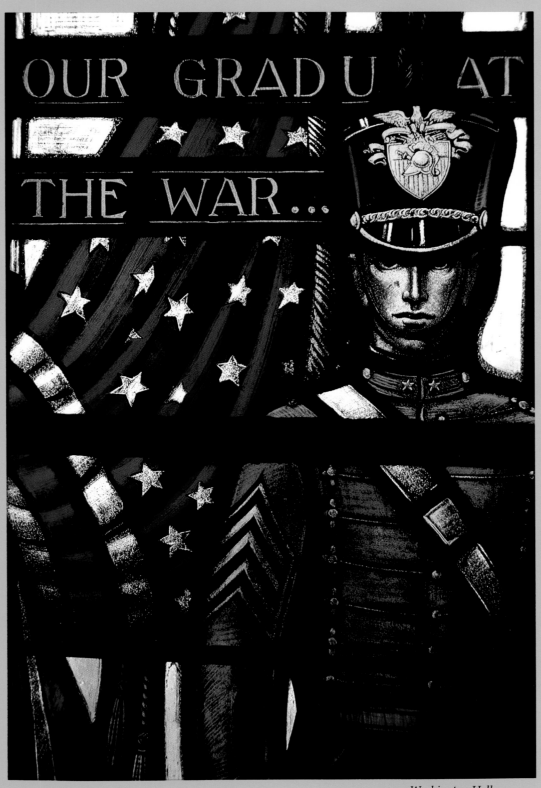

Washington Hall

1802 The United States Military Academy established by an Act of Congress. The Law directed that the Corps of Engineers "shall constitute a Military Academy." The West Point site was selected because of economy, convenience, and its historically rich association with the American Revolution.

1812 Act of Congress enlarged the Academy, set entrance requirements and qualifications for cadets.

1816 Gray adopted as the color of the cadet uniform. The adoption of the new uniform was later said to be in honor of the victory of Winfield Scott's gray-clad Regulars at the battle of Chippewa.

1817 Sylvanus Thayer, an 1808 graduate, took command of the Military Academy. Thayer established the principle of strict adherence to the rule of discipline and advancement according to merit as basic to a military education.

1820 Superintendent's Quarters completed. Colonel Thayer was the first Superintendent to live there.

1828 Kosciusko Monument given by the Corps of Cadets in honor of Colonel Thaddeus Kosciusko, who helped plan the fortifications at West Point during the Revolutionary War.

1838 An Act of Congress made the term of service eight years thus ensuring to the government four years of service in return for the four years of education.

1843 Congress passed a law providing for one cadet from each Congressional district.

1845 New Barracks begun that constitute a section of what was later known as Central Barracks.

1848 Military successes in the Mexican War established national confidence in West Point training. Winfield Scott praised the Military Academy in the enunciation of his famous "fixed opinion."

1852 New Mess Hall (later renamed Grant Hall) was completed.

1861 Academy provided over 400 generals to lead both North and South in the Civil War.

1866 Act of Congress provided that the Superintendent of the Military Academy may "hereafter be selected, and the officers on duty at the institution detailed from any arm of the service." The law recognized the fact that the Academy was no longer a school of engineering and it removed the control of the institution from the Corps of Engineers.

1868 The formal dedication and unveiling of the statue erected in the memory of Major General John Sedgwick, commander of the Sixth Army Corps, who fell in the Battle of Spotsylvania.

1869 Meeting held to organize the Association of Graduates of the United States Military Academy, helping to bring the North and the South together after the Civil War.

1883 Thayer Monument dedicated to Colonel Sylvanus Thayer, the "Father of the Military Academy." Dedication address by Major General George W. Cullum.

1890 First Army-Navy football game. The Military Academy enters the field of intercollegiate athletics.

1895 West Academic Building completed.

1897 Battle Monument dedicated. Designed by Stanford White, executed by Frederic MacMonnies. Located at Trophy Point at the northern limit of the Plain, it is dedicated to the memory of the 2,240 soldiers and officers of the Regular Army killed in action in the Civil War.

1898 Coat of Arms and Academy seal adopted. Cullum Memorial Hall completed. Named after Major General George W. Cullum, United States Military Academy 1833, Superintendent, 1864-1866.

1899 The colors black, gray and gold were adopted as the colors of the United States Military Academy for the use in all athletic games. Elihu Root, Secretary of War , praised the Academy's contribution in the Spanish-American War: "I believe that the great service which it has rendered the country was never more conspicuous than it has been during the past two years."

1902 The Military Academy Centennial. Observed with President Theodore Roosevelt as the guest of honor. "The Corps," the Academy's inspiring anthem, was written for the Centennial by Herbert S. Shipman, United States Military Academy Chaplain.

UNITED STATES MILITARY

1903 West Point Army Mess (the Officers' Club) was completed.

1908 North Barracks completed.

1909 Constitution Island donated to the government (West Point) by Mrs. Russell Sage and Miss Anna B. Warner. Administration Building completed.

1910 Cadet Chapel completed. East Gymnasium completed.

1911 Riding Hall completed. "Alma Mater" first sung as hymn.

1913 East Academic Building completed.

1916 Washington Monument completed. It is a replica of the Washington Monument in Union Square, New York City.

1917 Academy graduates serve as 34 of the 38 Corps and Division Commanders in the First World War.

1919 French Cadet Monument erected. Presented by the cadets of L'Ecole Polytechnique.

1920 General MacArthur assumes Superintendency. Under his direction the course of instruction was reviewed and modernized. He also established intramural athletics for all classes. He wrote the couplet: "Upon the fields of friendly strife are sown the seeds that, upon other fields on other days will bear the fruits of victory." Major Robert M. Danford, Commandant of Cadets, introduced a course on leadership. As an aid in the appointment of cadet officers and noncommissioned officers in a greatly enlarged Corps, he devised and utilized a system of efficiency ratings of cadets by cadets.

1924 Michie Stadium completed. Football stadium named for 1st Lt. Dennis Mahan Michie, United States Military Academy 1892, captain of the first West Point football team, killed in action at San Juan, Cuba in 1898.

1933 Act of Congress authorized awarding the Bachelor of Science degree to Academy graduates.

1939 Doubleday Field named in honor of Major General Abner Doubleday, United States Military Academy 1842, who is said to have laid out the first modern baseball diamond at Cooperstown, New York in 1839.

1941 Academy graduates such as Eisenhower, MacArthur, Bradley and Patton began leading Allies to victory in World War II.

1946 Under Major General Maxwell D. Taylor, Superintendent, the curriculum was carefully and thoroughly revised and modernized.

1950 The George S. Patton, Jr. Monument unveiled and dedicated. This monument was "erected by his friends, officers and men of the units he commanded."

1956 Conversion of the Riding Hall to an academic building. (Thayer Hall) begun.

1960 United States Military Academy recognized as an official national historical landmark.

1962 On May 12, General of the Army, Douglas MacArthur, accepted the Thayer Award and delivered his famous "Duty, Honor, Country" speech.

1964 President Johnson signed law which resulted in an Academy expansion program almost doubling the strength of the Corps by 1973. New Library dedicated.

1965 Colonel Edward H. White II, United States Military Academy 1952, became first American to walk in space.

1969 MacArthur Memorial and Barracks dedicated.

1972 New Cadet Activities Center dedicated as Eisenhower Hall.

1973 Cavalry Plain renamed Buffalo Soldier Field.

1976 Women cadets entered the Military Academy.

1983 Eisenhower Monument dedicated.

1984 Academy acquired former Ladycliff College (New South Post) property.

1985 New Sports Center completed.

ACADEMY MILESTONES

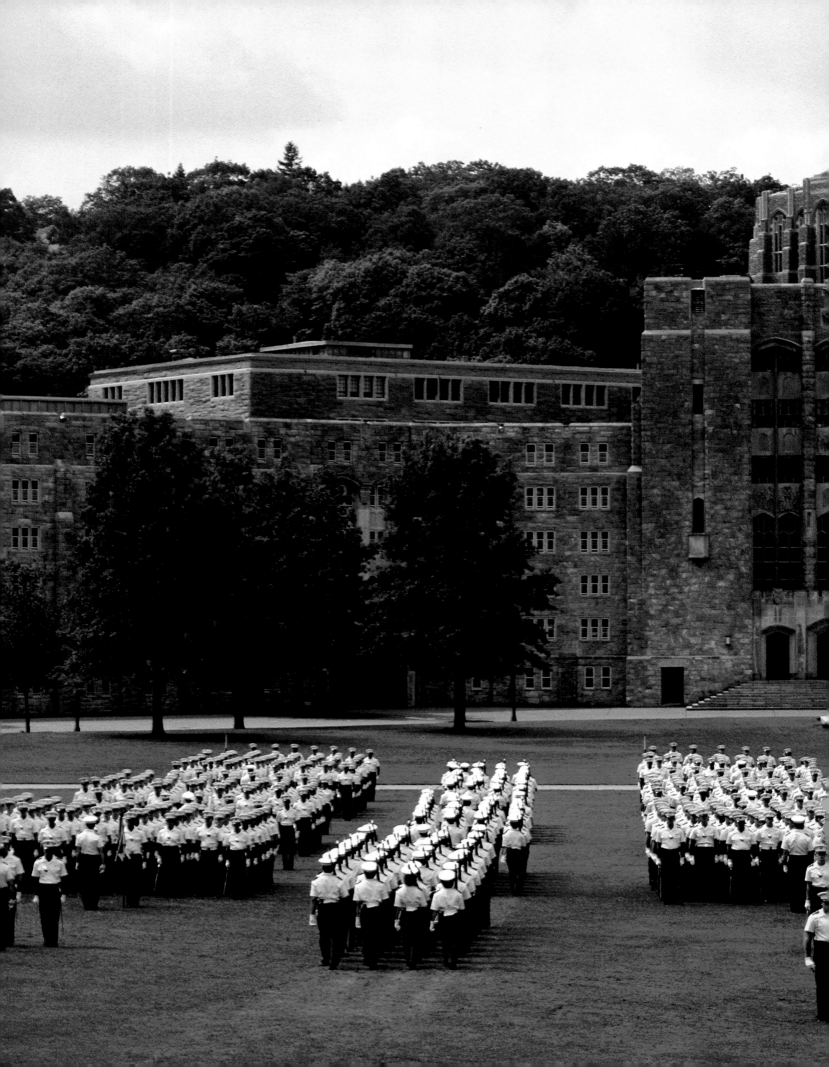

When you decided to follow the soldiers' profession, you sought admission to the soldiers' university. You came to study in one of the world's most beautiful places, whose very surroundings and traditions are enough to inspire the least emotional. Even the casual tourist cannot visit this picturesque site on the wooded banks of the Hudson without being uplifted by these historical associations, this atmosphere of dedication to high purpose, the traditions that invest old West Point with the storied glamour of a glamorous past.

James W. Good, Secretary of War, address June 1929

Eisenhower Barracks

Battle Monument

Overleaf: Trophy Point Amphitheatre

Reception Day

You have been selected and are maintained at public cost not for what you have done, but for what you are to do; not for deeds of great benefit to the State already performed, but for services you are expected hereafter to render. By entering this Academy, and becoming the recipients of the thorough instruction here imparted, you have incurred the most weighty and solemn obligations. You have no longer the privilege of common citizens to live and die obscurely.

Ashbel Smith, address 1848

Cadet Mess, Washington Hall

West Point takes the richest and the poorest, the farmer's son and the factory worker's boy, from all walks of life and gives them an excellent academic education and unparalleled opportunity for service to their country. The leadership training at West Point is typically democratic, typically American and All-American. For 150 years West Point has graduated men in whom America and the Armed Forces can take great pride.

General Omar Bradley, Chairman Joint Chiefs of Staff, Founders Day, 1952

Whatever argument may be drawn from particular examples…a thorough examination of the subject will envince that the art of war is at once comprehensive and complicated, that it demands much previous study, and that the possession of it in its most improved and perfect state is always of great moment to the security of a nation. This, therefore, ought to be a serious care of every government; – and for this purpose, an Academy where a regular course of instruction is given, is an obvious expedient which different nations have successfully employed.

George Washington, his Eighth Message.

Math Class

General Grant Portrait / Library

Overleaf: Mural, Washington Hall **41**

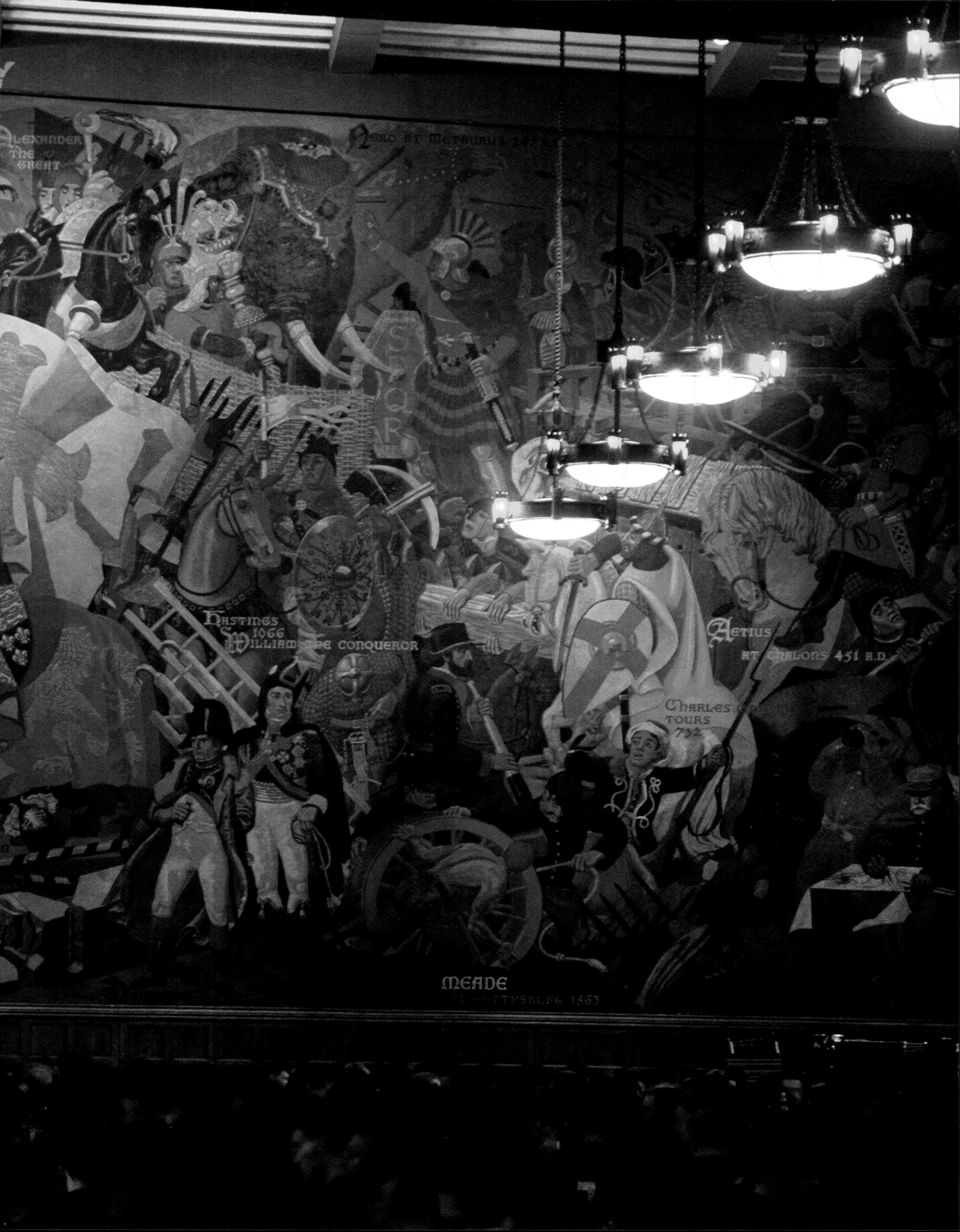
ALEXANDER THE GREAT
HASTINGS 1066
AETIUS
TOURS 732
MEADE

Minute Caller

In no way can the designed effects of this institution be more effectually realized than by a steady, persevering, inflexible, conscientious obedience to all its requisitions. Remember that no rule, order or regulation can be intentionally evaded...no demand of duty can be designedly disregarded, without weakening that habit of obedience, which is the first duty, the highest honor of a soldier.

Ivers J. Austin, address, June 1842

If you have to fight, may you experience the two most delightful moments that a man can have in this life. The first is when he knows that he is doing what the enemy did not expect him to do. And the other is when, after a hard fight, he hears the shout of victory, sees the flag floating above him, and knows that another laurel is added to the credit of American arms. Either one of these moments will repay a lifetime's labors and cares.

Lt. Gen. Nelson A. Miles, speech, June 1902

Retreat

Though relatively small in numbers, men of West Point have always been the leaven and have ever given the guiding impulse that has carried our armies to victory... No other institution has furnished to the country as great a proportion of distinguished citizens as West Point.

General John Pershing, address, June 1920

Recreation Of Late 1800's Cadet Period Room

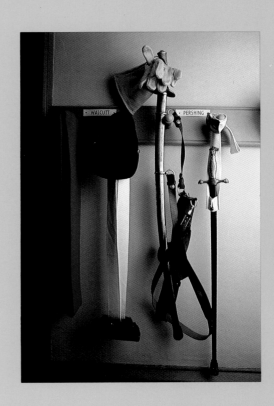

Cadet Period Room (Early 1900s)

Cadet Period Room (1960s)

Having visited a great many universities in the U.S. in the last 20 years, I should like to testify to the fact that I have seldom, if ever, encountered a group of students who struck me as better disciplined intellectually for the study of international politics.

Sir Alfred Zimmern

Overleaf: Computer Assisted Terrain Analysis

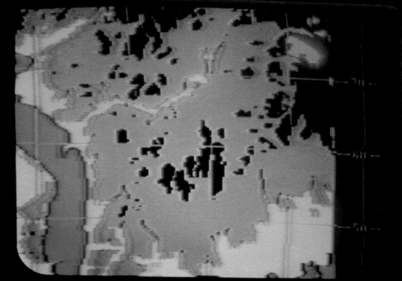

*Upon the fields of friendly strife are sown the seeds
That, upon other fields, on other days, will bear the fruits of victory.*

Carved in stone at the entrance to the gym, upon instruction
of Superintendent Douglas MacArthur, 1920

Retreat

This Academy and its sister school of Annapolis [are] the personification of democracy in the equality of opportunity they afford, uninfluenced by prior social position or economic standing. They nurture patriotism and devotion to country. They teach that honor, integrity and the faithful performance of duty are to be valued above all personal advantage or advancement. Their success is written in the long and brilliant record of service which their graduates rendered to the nation.

Franklin D. Roosevelt, graduation, 1935

Flirtation Walk

Cadet Chapel

An American officer, intelligent, refined, brave, accomplished in his profession, and with all this a faithful soldier and servant of Christ, is one of those specimens of our nature which we cannot behold without admiration, nor mention without praise.

Rev. J.W. French, speech, 1857

Jewish Chapel

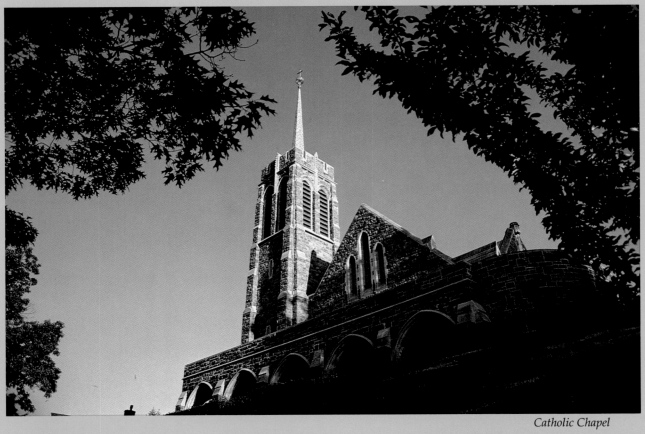

Catholic Chapel

The determinate West Point that is to be his master for four years and the shaper of his destiny meets him at the top of the slope with ominous silence. He hears no voice, he sees no portentous figure; but there is communicated in some way, through some medium, the presence of an invisible authority, cold, inexorable and relentless. Time never wears away this first feeling; it comes back to every graduate on returning to West Point, let his years and his honors be what they may.

Morris Schaff, in *The Spirit of Old West Point, 1858-1862*

Old Cadet Chapel

Clock Tower

Summer Training

The inspiration you will find on revisiting this place is even more stirring than that of a son returning home. The pulse quickens to the feeling that here is enshrined something of the selflessness of all the men who have fought and died for our country. Their spirit charges that our own work be no less devoted. It fires our purpose that this nation shall ever remain secure as it steadfastly pursues its far-reaching efforts toward man's betterment.

President Dwight D. Eisenhower

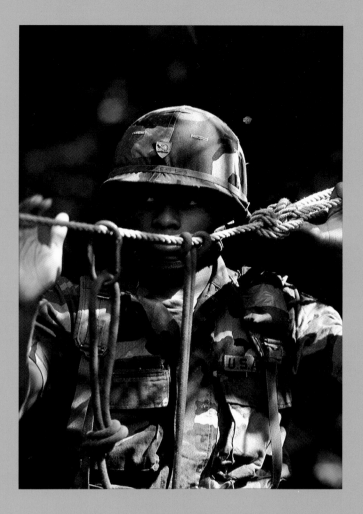

Recognition

The Academy has equipped you mentally, morally, physically and professionally for the most one can assume. From now on you must develop yourself and increase your value to the nation. Assume your duties in the knowledge that you are dealing with the lives of men and that nothing short of superlative effort can ever be tolerated.

General Omar N. Bradley, address, June 1945

We do not return to view again the massive gothic structures rising from the Plain, as impressive as they may be. We do not return to sit again at the feet of great teachers, even though they created the academic atmosphere which pervades West Point. We do come back because in the presence of the Corps, we feel again its deep, indefinable spirit of service. Only the Corps of Cadets has for 150 years received the heritages of the past, molded them to the present, and carried them forward as the traditions for the future.

General Lucius D. Clay, Sesquicentennial speech, 1952

Alumni Exercises

Alumni Review

You are about to leave this beautiful place, surrounded by a magnificent scenery, which should reflect its noble imagery in the mirror of your own minds... All those scenes and objects you are about to quit, perhaps forever. The moment of freedom from academic restraints may appear to you for a moment full of joy and enthusiasm. You will cast, I know, a "long lingering look behind" when you leave the Academy at West Point, but go "where duty calls you," and improve, as I know you will, the advantages you have enjoyed.

Thomas B. Reed, graduation, June 1827

The grandest thing at West Point is a living concept –
the enduring idea that service to country matters.

Dave R. Palmer, Lieutenant General, U.S. Army
Superintendent, United States Military Academy

General Douglas MacArthur

This address was given by General of the Army Douglas MacArthur to the Members of the Association of Graduates, U.S.M.A., The Corps of Cadets and Distinguished Guests upon his acceptance of The Sylvanus Thayer Award, United States Military Academy, West Point, New York, 12 May 1962.

General Westmoreland, General Groves, distinguished guests, and gentlemen of the Corps:

As I was leaving the hotel this morning, a doorman asked me, "Where are you bound for, General?" and when I replied, "West Point," he remarked, "Beautiful place, have you been there before?"

No human being could fail to be deeply moved by such a tribute as this (Thayer Award). Coming from a profession I have served so long, and a people I have loved so well, it fills me with an emotion I cannot express. But this award is not intended primarily to honor a personality, but to symbolize a great moral code — the code of conduct and chivalry of those who guard this beloved land of culture and ancient descent. This is the meaning of the medallion. For all eyes and for all time, it is an expression of the ethics of the American soldier. That I should be integrated in this way with so noble an ideal arouses a sense of pride and yet of humility which will be with me always.

Duty - Honor - Country. Those three hallowed words reverently dictate what you ought to be, what you can be, what you will be. They are your rallying points: to build courage when courage seems to fail; to regain faith when there seems to be little faith; to create hope when hope becomes forlorn. Unhappily, I possess neither that eloquence of diction, that poetry of imagination, nor that brilliance of metaphor to tell you all they mean. The unbelievers will say they are but words, but a slogan, but a flamboyant phrase. Every pedant, every demagogue, every cynic, every hypocrite, every troublemaker, and I am sorry to say, some others of an entirely different character, will try to downgrade them even to the extent of mockery and ridicule. But these are some of the things they do. They build your basic character, they mold you for your future roles as the custodians of the nation's defense, they make you strong enough to know when you are weak, and brave enough to face yourself when you are afraid. They teach you to be proud and unbending in honest failure, but humble and gentle in success; not to substitute words for actions, nor to seek the path of comfort, but to face the stress and spur of difficulty and challenge; to learn to stand up in the storm but to have compassion on those who fall; to master yourself before you seek to master others; to have a heart that is clean, a goal that is high; to learn to laugh yet never forget how to weep; to reach into the future yet never neglect the past; to be serious yet never to take yourself too seriously; to be modest so that you will remember the simplicity of true greatness, the open mind of true wisdom, the meekness of true strength. They give you a temper of the will, a quality of the imagination, a vigor of the emotions, a freshness of the deep springs of life, a temperamental predominance of courage over timidity, an appetite for adventure over love of ease. They create in your heart the sense of wonder, the unfailing hope of what next, and the joy and inspiration of life. They teach you in this way to be an officer and a gentleman.

And what sort of soldiers are those you are to lead? Are they reliable, are they brave, are they capable of victory? Their story is known to all of you; it is the story of the American man-at-arms. My estimate of him was formed on the battlefield many, many years ago, and has never changed. I regarded him then as I regard him now — as one of the world's noblest figures, not only as one of the finest military characters but also as one of the most stainless. His name and fame are the birthright of every American citizen. In his youth and strength, his love and loyalty he gave — all that mortality can give. He needs no eulogy from me or from any other man. He has written his own history and written it in red on his enemy's breast. But when I think of his patience under adversity, of his courage under fire, and of his modesty in victory, I am filled with an emotion of admiration I cannot put into words. He belongs to history as furnishing one of the greatest examples of successful patriotism; he belongs to posterity as the instructor of future generations in the principles of liberty and freedom; he belongs to the present, to us, by his virtues and by his achievements. In 20 campaigns, on a hundred battlefields, around a thousand campfires, I have witnessed

General George Washington

that enduring fortitude, that patriotic self-abnegation and that invincible determination which have carved his statue in the hearts of his people. From one end of the world to the other he has drained deep the chalice of courage.

As I listened to those songs of the glee club, in memory's eye I could see those staggering columns of the First World War, bending under soggy packs, on many a weary march from dripping dusk to drizzling dawn, slogging ankle-deep through the mire of shell-shocked roads, to form grimly for the attack, blue-lipped, covered with sludge and mud, chilled by the wind and rain; driving home to their objective, and,

for many, to the judgement seat of God. I do not know the dignity of their birth but I do know the glory of their death. They died unquestioning, uncomplaining, with faith in their hearts, and on their lips the hope that would go on to victory. Always for them — Duty - Honor - Country; always their blood and sweat and tears as we sought the way and the light and the truth.

And 20 years after, on the other side of the globe, again the filth of murky foxholes, the stench of ghostly trenches, the slime of dripping dugouts; those boiling suns of relentless heat, those torrential rains of devastating storms; the loneliness and utter desolation of jungle trails, the bitterness of long separation from those they loved and cherished, the deadly pestilence of tropical disease, the horror of stricken areas of war; their resolute and determined defense, their swift and sure attack, their indomitable purpose, their complete and decisive victory — always victory. Always through the bloody haze of their last reverberating shot, the vision of gaunt, ghastly men reverently following your password of Duty - Honor - Country. The code which those words perpetuate embraces the highest moral laws and will stand the test of any ethics or philosophies ever promulgated for the uplift of mankind.

Its requirements are for the things that are right, and its restraints are from the things that are wrong. The soldier, above all other men, is required to practice the greatest act of religious training — sacrifice. In battle and in the face of danger and death, he discloses those divine attributes which his Maker gave when he created man in his own image. No physical courage and no brute instinct can take the place of the Divine help which alone can sustain him. However horrible the incidents of war may be, the soldier who is called upon to offer and to give his life for his country, is the noblest development of mankind.

You now face a new world — a world of change. The thrust into outer space of the satellite, spheres and missiles marked the beginning of another epoch in the long story of mankind — the chapter of the space age. In the five or more billions of years the scientists tell us it has taken to form the earth, in the three or more billion years of development of the human race, there has never been a greater, a more abrupt or staggering evolution. We deal now not with things of this world alone, but with the illimitable distances and as yet unfathomed mysteries of the universe. We are reaching out for a new and boundless frontier. We speak in

Old Cadet Chapel Graveyard

strange terms; of harnessing the cosmic energy; of making winds and tides work for us; of creating unheard synthetic materials to supplement or even replace our old standard basics; of purifying sea water for our drink; of mining ocean floors for new fields of wealth and food; of disease preventatives to expand life into the hundreds of years; on controlling the weather for a more equitable distribution of heat and cold, or rain and shine, of space ships to the moon; of the primary target in war, no longer limited to the armed forces of any enemy, but instead to include his civil populations; of ultimate conflict between a united human race and the sinister forces of some other planetary galaxy; of such dreams and fantasies as to make life the most exciting of all time.

And through all this welter of change and development, your mission remains fixed, determined, inviolable — it is to win our wars. Everything else in your professional career is but corollary to this vital dedication. All other public purposes, all other public proj-

ects, all other public needs, great or small, will find others for their accomplishment; but you are the ones who are trained to fight: yours is the profession of arms — the will to win, the sure knowledge that in war there is no substitue for victory; that if you lose, the nation will be destroyed; that the very obsession of your public service must be Duty - Honor - Country. Others will debate the controversial issues, national and international, which divide men's minds; but serene, calm, aloof, you stand as the nation's war-guardian, as its lifeguard from the raging tides of international conflict, as its gladiator in the arena of battle. For a century and a half you have defended, guarded, and protected its hallowed traditions of liberty and freedom, of right and justice. Let civilian voices argue the merits or demerits of our processes of government; whether our strength is being sapped by deficit financing, indulged in too long, by federal paternalism grown too mighty, by power groups grown too arrogant, by politics grown too corrupt, by crime grown too rampant, by morals grown too low, by taxes grown too high, by extremists grown too violent; whether our personal liberties are as thorough and complete as they should be. These great national problems are not for your professional participation or military solution. Your guidepost stands out like a ten-fold beacon in the night — Duty - Honor - Country. You are the leaven which binds together the entire fabric of our national system of defense. From your ranks come the great captains who hold the nation's destiny in their hands the moment the war tocsin sounds. The Long Gray Line has never failed us. Were you to do so, a million ghosts in olive drab, in brown khaki, in blue and gray, would rise from their white crosses thundering those magic words — Duty - Honor - Country. This does not mean that you are war mongers. On the contrary, the soldier, above all other people, prays for peace, for they must suffer and bear the deepest wounds and scars of war. But always in our ears ring the ominous words of Plato, that wisest of all philosophers, "Only the dead have seen the end of war."

The shadows are lengthening for me. The twilight is here. My days of old have vanished tone and tint; they have gone glimmering through the dreams of things that were. Their memory is one of wondrous beauty, watered by tears, and coaxed and caressed by the smiles of yesterday. I listen vainly for the witching melody of faint bugles blowing reveille, of far drums beating the long roll. In my dreams I hear again the crash of guns, the rattle of musketry, the strange, mournful mutter of the battlefield.

But in the evening of my memory, always I come back to West Point. Always there echoes and reechoes Duty - Honor - Country.

Today marks my final roll call with you, but I want you to know that when I cross the river my last conscious thoughts will be of The Corps, and The Corps, and The Corps.

I bid you farewell.

General Dwight D. Eisenhower